THE MICROSOFT MONOPOLY CONTROVERSY

A Historical Analysis of Whether Microsoft Was an Illegal
Monopoly in the 1990s

JANUARY 29, 2016

SCOTT A STAWSKI

Copyright 2016 by Scott Stawski
Prosper, Texas 75078

www.scottstawski.com

For inquiries, please contact sastawski@gmail.com.

Company and product names mentioned herein are the trademarks or registered trademarks of their respective owners.

All rights reserved. No part of this book may be reproduced, in any form or by any means, without permission in writing from the author.

Printed in the United States of America

First Printing February 2016

ISBN-13: 978-1523843602
ISBN-10: 1523843608

Table of Contents

About the Author

Scott A. Stawski is an Author and an Executive for Hewlett Packard Enterprise (HPE). Scott is responsible for managing the sales and revenue generation activities for HPE's largest and most strategic global accounts, exceeding $500M in revenue annually.

Scott brings a wealth of experience in business outcome-based technology service delivery. He has led numerous multimillion-dollar business intelligence and technology solutions and strategy engagements for Global 500 companies within the health and life science; manufacturing and technology; retail; travel; communication, media, and entertainment; and consumer packaged goods sectors.

Prior to joining Hewlett Packard, Scott was a Senior Principal at Knightsbridge, a leading business intelligence consultancy acquired by Hewlett Packard, where he developed business intelligence strategies and platforms for Fortune 500 companies.

Before entering technology consulting, Scott held executive and management positions at the CRM consultancy Inforte and newspaper chain Knight Ridder.

A trusted advisor for CEOs, CFOs, and CIOs in the Americas, Scott is a recognized expert in analytics and data management, technology strategy, outsourcing, and next-generation application transformation to the cloud. He is the Author of *Inflection Point: How the Convergence of Cloud, Mobility, Apps, and Data Will Shape the Future of Business* published by Pearson FT Press. A contributing writer for leading media outlets including TheStreet.com, Scott is a speaker and facilitator at many of the leading industry shows and conferences and is frequently interviewed and quoted by leading media outlets, including *The Economist*, *The Chicago Tribune*, *San Francisco Chronicle*, *Editor & Publisher*, *Crain's Chicago Business*, and *National Public Radio*.

Scott is also Secretary of the Board for the Celina Economic Development Council and active with ChildFund International and Shakespeare Dallas and is working towards his Master of Liberal Arts, Extension Studies at Harvard University.

Foreword

As one African proverb explains, "Until lions have their historians, tales of the hunt shall always glorify the hunters." Not unlike social, cultural or political history, the history of business is fraught with historical controversies. Those entering the business world today will be faced with enormous challenges including technology innovation that is disrupting many business sectors. As an example, the largest hospitality company in the world today, Airbnb.com, does not own a single hotel room. The largest livery company in the world, Uber, does not own a single taxi cab. And, both companies did not exist five years ago. Uber is rapidly displacing many traditional taxicab companies in many cities. Does Uber's success equate to being a monopoly with abusive practices?

The topic of the Microsoft monopoly controversy of the 1990's was chosen not merely for an academic exercise. Major disruption is occurring driven by the convergence of technology including cloud, software as a service, and mobility. Some existing technology providers are thriving and others are struggling. New entrants in the marketplace are at times so disruptive, they create new technical paradigms and business models that rapidly replace entire existing sectors. Some might see some of these companies as illegal monopolies. Is Amazon Web Services an illegal monopoly for cloud services? Or Google for online search?

From 1969 to 1982, the U.S. government spent countless dollars and bandwidth on an antitrust probe of IBM.[1] That stopped in the 1980s as it was hard to investigate IBM for monopolistic activity when it was struggling due to its inability to keep up with innovation in the PC and software market. Intel spent the 1990s and 2000s fighting similar antitrust actions only to see their market share erode as the market for chips switched from servers and PCs to mobile devices. The focus of this paper is the similar review of accusations of illegal monopolistic practices by Microsoft in the 1990s. Fast forward 15 years, in 2014 Microsoft announced the layoff of 18,000 employees or 14% of its workforce.[2] Were they really a monopoly in 1998?

---

[1] CNet, "IBM and Microsoft: Antitrust then and now", http://www.cnet.com/news/ibm-and-microsoft-antitrust-then-and-now/ (January 2, 2002).
[2] Clay, Kelly, Forbes, "Why Microsoft's Layoff Is Much More Sweeping Than The 18,000 Cuts" http://www.forbes.com/sites/kellyclay/2014/07/20/microsoft-layoffs-also-impact-thousands-of-contractors/#2715e4857a0be9941dc2c11a (July 20, 2014).

The broader significance of this paper is that we need to understand that our way of thinking about antitrust, monopoly, and anticompetitive practices must change, as well as the laws codifying this thinking. The laws that were created specifically to curb anticompetitive behavior in stable, low innovation areas are not applicable in today's disruptive, innovative environment where entire markets are redefined in months. Therefore, the Microsoft controversy is an important topic for debate.

Introduction

The focus of this research project is to provide a review and analysis on the controversy of whether Microsoft was an illegal monopoly that stifled competition during the late 1990's and early 2000's. Microsoft was founded by Bill Gates and Paul Allen on April 4, 1975.[3] As of September 20, 2015, Microsoft had annual revenue of $90.76 billion, more than 118,000 employees and a market valuation of $359.98 billion[4]. It is the 25th largest company in the world. In many circles, Microsoft is well regarded. USA Today ranked Microsoft 5th in their January 2015 article, *The world's most innovative companies*. Bill Gates himself stated in 1991, "Microsoft is not about greed. It's about innovation and fairness."[5] However, on May 18, 1998 the United States Department of Justice and 20 individual States sued Microsoft accusing the company of being an illegal monopoly and engaging in abusive practices.[6] Subsequently, Microsoft was accused and found liable for

---

[3] "Microsoft", New World Encyclopedia, http://www.newworldencyclopedia.org/p/index.php?title=Microsoft&oldid=980539, (January 22, 2016).
[4] "MSFT", Yahoo Finance, http://finance.yahoo.com/q/ks?s=MSFT+Key+Statistics, (November 2, 2015).
[5] Bill Gates, "Bill Gates on Microsoft, FT.com, http://www.ft.com/cms/s/2/1674298c-fcbe-11da-9599-0000779e2340.html (June 15, 2006).
[6] United States of America, Appellee v. Microsoft Corporation, Appellant, 253

monopolistic practices by the European Commission in 2004, South Korea in 2005 and again by the European Commission in 2008.[7]

Was Microsoft an illegal monopoly that engaged in abusive practices during the late 1990's and early 2000's? The debate as to whether Microsoft was an illegal monopoly continues to this day. Microsoft has received much media coverage surrounding the legal cases both in the United States and Europe. This media coverage and some of the initial legal findings concluded that Microsoft was an illegal monopoly with abusive practices. The frequency of this assertion has resulted in a de facto belief in its truth in some circles. However, others cite subsequent legal decisions as well as new developments in the industry over the past decade to assert that Microsoft was not an illegal monopoly, but merely a successful innovator. These advocates believe that Microsoft has a place in history, that it was central to both the PC and the Internet revolutions and that the monopolistic fervor against Microsoft in the 1990s is a cautionary lesson about judicial overreach in a business sector the courts do not understand. The

F.3d 34 (D.C. Cir. 2001), Justia U.S. Law, http://law.justia.com/cases/federal/appellate-courts/F3/253/34/576095/, (December 30, 2015).
[7] Wikipedia contributors, "Microsoft litigation", Wikipedia, https://en.wikipedia.org/wiki/Microsoft_litigation#Anti-trust (December 2, 2015).

research paper reviews arguments on both sides of the controversy and explores the hypothesis that Microsoft was not an illegal monopoly that relied on abusive, anticompetitive practices during the late 1990s and early 2000s. To test this hypothesis, I will address the following sub-questions:

- What is the definition of a monopoly?
- What is the relationship between a monopoly and anticompetitive practices?
- How have governments reacted to the question of whether Microsoft was a monopoly? What was the eventual outcome of the legal proceedings?
- As time has passed, what new evidence has emerged that is relevant to the discussion of Microsoft's alleged monopolistic practices in the 1990's and 2000's?
- What is the significance of the Microsoft monopoly controversy?

Upon review, I conclude that Microsoft was not as an illegal monopoly that relied on abusive, anticompetitive practices during the late 1990s and early 2000s. Many of the legal verdicts that concluded Microsoft was an illegal monopoly were either overturned or the legal remedy was not implemented due to changing market conditions. The evidence that Microsoft had no competition and/or utilized its market share to stifle competition is not supported by the evidence. Lastly, history has shown that Microsoft had intense competition that ultimately has resulted in Microsoft's loss of leading market share to other competitors.

Definition of Monopoly

An accepted legal definition of monopoly is: "An economic advantage held by one or more persons or companies deriving from the exclusive power to carry on a particular business or trade or to manufacture and sell a particular item, thereby suppressing competition and allowing such persons or companies to raise the price of a product or service substantially above the price that would be established by a free market."[8]

In a monopoly, a single seller or producer supplies a product or service for a market. They enjoy an exclusive and/or dominant market share.[9] A company is said to be a monopoly if there are no realistic substitutes for the product or service offered, and there is no realistic chance of a competitor to enter the market. In this scenario, the company with the monopoly is able to set the price with virtually no marketplace pressures. In order for a company to establish a

---

[8] Collins Dictionary of Law. S.v. "monopoly", http://legal-dictionary.thefreedictionary.com/monopoly (December 3, 2015).
[9] Funk & Wagnalls Encyclopedia. "Monopoly", http://www.cosmeo.com (November 30, 2015).

monopoly, it must be able to acquire one or more of the following

advantages:[10]

1. Control of the major source or ingredient that is necessary to manufacture the product;
2. A proprietary technology allowing the company to produce a product or service that no other firm can duplicate. This situation is often referred to as a *natural* monopoly;
3. An exclusive patent for a product or the processes used to manufacture that product; and
4. A government sanctioned arrangement that provides a company the exclusive right to produce a product or service for a specific market. For example, the U.S. government has granted Major League Baseball an exemption to monopoly regulations allowing it to be the only national, professional baseball entity.

It is important to note that a company is not an unlawful

monopoly simply by having a dominant market share within a sector

through either lower pricing, a superior product or service or even

vigorous competition. Globally, countries have various legal

regulations defining and restricting illegal monopolies. The defining

characteristic of these laws regardless of country, is that <u>to be</u>

<u>considered an unlawful monopoly, a company must suppress</u>

<u>competition with anticompetitive behavior</u>. The U.S Department of

---

[10] American University, "Protecting Competition or Competitors? The Government's Double Edged Sword", http://www1.american.edu/projects/mandala/TED/smith/Greenspoon.htm (December 14, 2015).

Justice states that an unlawful monopoly exists when, "one firm controls the market for a product or service, and it has obtained that market power, not because its product or service is superior to others, but by suppressing competition with anticompetitive conduct."[11]

Over the years, the United States government has enacted a series of laws establishing the legal framework relating to illegal monopolies. I will review this legislation briefly before delving into nature of the Microsoft controversy.

In the latter part of the nineteenth century, abusive monopolistic practices became widespread, particularly in the railroad industry. [12] Congress took action in 1887, passing the Interstate Commerce Act.[13] At that time, the competition between railroad companies for long-haul routes was vigorous. However, the competition for short-haul runs was not. As a result, railroads provided rebates for short-haul runs to large shippers, in order to keep their long-haul business. This discriminatory pricing method was

---

[11] United States Department of Justice, "Antitrust Laws and You", http://www.justice.gov/atr/antitrust-laws-and-you (December 3, 2015).

[12] Law Library - American Law and Legal Information, "Monopoly – Government Regulation", http://law.jrank.org/pages/8632/Monopoly-Government-Regulation.html (December 15, 2015).

[13] Law Library, see footnote 10

particularly harmful to farmers because they did not have the volume necessary to receive these rebates.[14] The Interstate Commerce Act was enacted as a legal basis to regulate shipping rates. It directed that rates be set equitably, and it made illegal unreasonable discrimination among shippers through the use of rebates or other discounts.[15]

The United States Congress passed the Sherman Antitrust Act in July 1890. The act made illegal "every contract, combination in the form of trust or otherwise, or conspiracy, in restraint of trade or commerce among the several States, or with foreign nations."[16] The Sherman Antitrust Act serves as the legal foundation by the United States government to ensure by legal means a competitive economic environment. The Act's basis is that "unrestrained competitive interaction yields the best allocation of our economic resources, the lowest prices, the highest quality and the greatest material progress, while at the same time providing an environment conducive to the preservation of our democratic, political and social institutions."[17]

---

[14] Law Library, see footnote 10
[15] Legal Information Institute, "U.S. Code: Title 49 - TRANSPORTATION ", https://www.law.cornell.edu/uscode/text/49/ (January 4, 2016).
[16] Legal Information Institute, "15 U.S. Code § 1 - Trusts, etc., in restraint of trade illegal; penalty", https://www.law.cornell.edu/uscode/text/15/1 (January 4, 2016).
[17] Kempf Jr., Donald G., The Seattle Times, "Antitrust Upside Down: The Microsoft Case." October 11 1999, page B5.

The Sherman Act gave a means for both criminal prosecution and civil penalties for anticompetitive behavior.[18]   In particular, the Act authorized tripling the amount of the damages awarded in a civil case. My analysis of the Act is that it was designed to encourage private parties to take action, which combined with possible government action further promotes a competitive environment and discourages violators from future anticompetitive activity.

The Clayton Antitrust Act was signed into law in 1914 and served to amend the Sherman Antitrust Act. The Clayton Antitrust Act outlawed such practices as price discrimination and forcing combined contracts, which required a buyer or seller to work exclusively with a specific company.[19] One of the main components of the Clayton legislation was defining "which acts were illegal but not criminal."[20] The act gave clarity to certain practices that were deemed illegal if they materially reduced competition or created a trade

---

[18] Federal Trade Commission, "The Antitrust Laws", https://www.ftc.gov/tips-advice/competition-guidance/guide-antitrust-laws/antitrust-laws (December 4, 2015).

[19] Editors of Encyclopædia Britannica, Encyclopaedia Britannica, "Clayton Antitrust Act", http://www.britannica.com/event/Clayton-Antitrust-Act (January 4, 2016).

[20] Law Library - American Law and Legal Information, "Monopoly – Government Regulation", http://law.jrank.org/pages/8632/Monopoly-Government-Regulation.html (December 15, 2015).

monopoly. Such practices included: price discrimination – selling an identical product at a different price to different competing buyers, exclusive-dealing contracts – selling a product or service with the condition that the buyer stop purchasing from its competitors, and corporate acquisitions and Board of Director overlap – appointing an individual to the Board of Directors of competing companies.

In order to establish an agency to enforce laws related to monopolistic practices and anticompetitive behavior, Congress passed the Federal Trade Commission Act of 1914.[21] The mission of the FTC is to "promote free and fair competitive trade in interstate commerce through the prohibition of price-fixing arrangements, false advertising, boycotts, illegal combinations of competitors, and other methods of unfair competition."[22]

In order to strengthen existing legislation on pricing abuses, Congress passed the Robinson-Patman Act in 1936.[23] This Act

---

[21] Legal Information Institute, "15 U.S. Code Subchapter I - FEDERAL TRADE COMMISSION", https://www.law.cornell.edu/uscode/text/15/chapter-2/subchapter-I (January 4, 2016).

[22] Law Library - American Law and Legal Information, "Monopoly – Government Regulation", http://law.jrank.org/pages/8632/Monopoly-Government-Regulation.html (December 15, 2015).

[23] Legal Information Institute, "15 U.S. Code § 13 - Discrimination in price, services, or facilities", https://www.law.cornell.edu/uscode/text/15/13 (January 4, 2016).

solidified the framework for anticompetitive pricing, making it illegal for any seller to discriminate in the price charged for a comparable product or service where the effect might injure, destroy, or prevent competition.

Over the years, the United States government has strengthened the legal framework making monopolies illegal. The Celler-Kefauver Act of 1950 modified the Clayton Antitrust Act. It established a legal basis to discourage certain mergers. Specifically, it was designed to stop mergers and/or the procurement of the assets of a company if the merger was designed merely to prevent or substantially lower competition.[24] Over the years there have been many challenges to these laws. However, The U.S. Supreme Court has been consistent on upholding challenges to these laws. This is shown in *United States v. Topco Assocs.*, 405 U.S. 596, 610 (1972) where the Supreme Court stated that the "antitrust laws in general, and the Sherman Act in particular, are the Magna Carta of free enterprise"[25]. The analysis shows that this

[24] Legal Information Institute, "15 U.S. Code § 12 - Definitions; short title", https://www.law.cornell.edu/uscode/text/15/12 (January 4, 2016).
[25] Justia U.S. Supreme Court, "United States v. Topco Assocs., Inc. 405 U.S. 596 (1972)", https://supreme.justia.com/cases/federal/us/405/596/ (January 4, 2016).

legal framework related to illegal monopolies are core to our society's

implementation of free, but regulated enterprise.

View 1: Microsoft was an illegal monopoly during the 1990s.

Microsoft was accused by competitors and various governments of being an illegal monopoly with abusive practices in the late 1990s and early 2000s. The accusations began with Microsoft's competitors including Apple, Sun, Netscape, and others. Steve Jobs, founder and CEO of Apple, stated in 1997 specific to Microsoft's monopoly "The ability to innovate in the industry has been sucked out dry and I think the smartest people have already seen the writing on the wall and started to exit. And I think some of the smartest young people are really questioning if they are even get in. Hopefully things will change over time but I think it's a dark period right now."[26] These accusations began to take hold in the public media. The headline story in the *Economist* on May 21, 1998 was *"At war with Microsoft"*.[27] The Independent Review summarizes the consensus headlines in the media at this time "From Capitol Hill to Silicon Valley, the computer software giant has been routinely denounced as a "monopolist"".[28] Soon the

[26] Steve Jobs, http://stevejobsdailyquote.com/2013/10/26/microsoft-monopoly/, January 25, 2016.
[27] Economist, "At war with Microsoft", http://www.economist.com/node/371844, May 21, 1998.
[28] Richard McKenzie. The Independent Review,

government quickly entered the controversy as seen with this *New York Times* headline on May 19, 1998 "U.S. And 20 States File Suits Claiming Microsoft".[29]

The widespread publicity surrounding those claims led to public perception that those accusations were and continue to be valid. Three primary arguments surface to the opinion that Microsoft was an illegal monopoly:

- Several legal bodies with standing have ruled Microsoft was an illegal monopoly,
- Microsoft's operating system and Internet Explorer have exclusive positioning in the marketplace creating an impossible barrier to entry, and
- Microsoft uses its dominant market position to implement abusive practices to eliminate competition and stifle innovation.

Several legal bodies with standing have ruled Microsoft was an illegal monopoly

The proponents that Microsoft was an illegal monopoly believe no controversy exists as the courts have ruled that Microsoft was an illegal monopoly. Richard McKenzie states in the fall of 1998, "The Microsoft monopoly is self-evident, if the Justice Department's lawyers

http://www.independent.org/publications/tir/article.asp?issueID=28&articleID=3
22, Fall 1998.
[29] Benton Foundation, https://www.benton.org/node/11820

are to be believed."[30] These proponents believe that if it can be established that Microsoft has been declared an illegal monopoly by recognized legal authorities, then Microsoft therefore was an illegal monopoly. The proponents believed the issue was resolved when U.S. District Judge Thomas Penfield Jackson declared Microsoft a monopoly in his findings of fact on November 5th 1999.[31] There is significant history with the issue prior to this finding.

<u>United States</u>

One of the earliest monopoly related cases brought against Microsoft occurred in 1994.[32] During the 1990s, Microsoft had in place with personal computer manufacturers (OEMs or original equipment manufacturers) what some called exclusionary licensing.[33] Microsoft required every manufacturer to pay for an MS-DOS license, even if the PC had installed an alternative operating system or if the

---

[30] McKenzie, p1

[31] *Wired Magazine*, "U.S. v. Microsoft: Timeline", http://www.wired.com/2002/11/u-s-v-microsoft-timeline/ (November 4, 2002).

[32] Lohr, Steve, *The New York Times*, "Judge Clears Antitrust Pact For Microsoft", http://www.nytimes.com/1995/08/22/business/judge-clears-antitrust-pact-for-microsoft.html (August 22, 1995). 1

[33] U.S. Dept of Justice, "MICROSOFT AGREES TO END UNFAIR MONOPOLISTIC PRACTICES", http://www.justice.gov/archive/opa/pr/Pre_96/July94/94387.txt.html (July 16, 1994)

end-user installed and used a non MS-DOS operating system. "Rivals

said this practice had chilled the market for competing software."[34]

Microsoft and the Justice Department agreed on a consent decree in

1994 and that decree was approved by Federal Judge Thomas P.

Jackson on August 21, 1995. "Microsoft agreed to a deal under which,

among other things, the company would not make the sale of its

operating systems conditional on the purchase of any other Microsoft

product."[35] The intent was for Microsoft to immediately stop bundling

Internet Explorer with Microsoft Windows. It was later expanded to

include Microsoft Media Player and Microsoft Office.[36] According to

the New York Times, at the time of the Consent decree between the

Justice Department and Microsoft, Microsoft had more than an 80

percent market share in personal computing operating systems.

Less than 3 years from the court approval of the above

Consent decree, 20 U.S. states and the Department of Justice

consolidated civil actions against Microsoft for illegal monopolistic

practices in the case *United States v. Microsoft*, 87 F. Supp. 2d 30 (D.D.C.

---

[34] Lohr, 1
[35] Lohr, 1
[36] Jeffrey A. Eisenach. Progress on Point, "The Microsoft Monopoly: The Facts, the Law and the Remedy", http://www.pff.org/issues-pubs/pops/pop7.4microsoftmonopolyfacts.html, April 2000.

2000). The premise of the case was that Microsoft used illegal

monopolistic activities to promote both its operating system sales and

its web browser sales.[37] At the core of the issue was Microsoft's

bundling of its Internet Explorer web browser with its Windows

operating system without requiring or even offering the ability to

purchase independently. The plaintiffs believed that this bundling

along with other anticompetitive practices allowed Microsoft to

squelch competition and achieve a dominant share of the web browser

market. The government's case specifically cite as example Microsoft's

ability to prevent OEM's from placing Netscape Navigator as a pre-

installed option on personal computers to compete with Microsoft's

Internet Explorer.[38]

The court through Judge Thomas Penfield Jackson released its

findings of fact on November 5, 1999. The court found that Microsoft

had violated the earlier consent decree between itself and the

Department of Justice.[39] The court further found that Microsoft's

[37] Kauffman, Kent, Legal Ethics (New York: Delmar Cengage Learning, 2008), p58-76.
[38] CNN, "Text of complaint in U.S. vs. Microsoft", http://www.cnn.com/US/9805/18/federal.complaint/ (May 18, 1998)
[39] John Frederick Moore. CNN Money, "MSFT ruled a monopoly", http://money.cnn.com/1999/11/05/technology/microsoft_finding/, (November 5, 1999).

dominance of the personal computer operating system market met the
definition of a monopoly and that Microsoft subsequently used that
monopoly for anticompetitive practices to eliminate or marginalize
competitors including Apple, Java, Netscape, Lotus Notes,
RealNetworks, Linux, and others.[40] Following the court releasing its
findings of fact, the court delivered its judgment and remedy. In April
of 2000, the courts judgement was that "Microsoft had committed
monopolization, attempted monopolization, and tying in violation of
Sections 1 and 2 of the Sherman Antitrust Act."[41] The court then
moved to the remedy stage of the trial. On June 7, 2000 the court
found that the only viable remedy was a breakup of Microsoft into two
independent businesses; a business to house the operating system and a
business to house the other software components including Internet
Explorer.[42]

The legal framework for illegal monopolies are very similar in
the U.S and Europe. "On the surface, there appears to be much in

[40] World Heritage Encyclopedia, "Microsoft litigation",
http://www.worldheritage.org/articles/Microsoft_litigation (December 15, 2015)
[41] Wired Magazine, "U.S. v. Microsoft: Timeline",
http://www.wired.com/2002/11/u-s-v-microsoft-timeline/ (November 4, 2002).
[42] Wired Magazine, "U.S. v. Microsoft: Timeline",
http://www.wired.com/2002/11/u-s-v-microsoft-timeline/ (November 4, 2002).

common between competition law in the United States and

competition law in the European Union."[43] Both countries embrace

the free market but have regulations to prevent one company's

dominant market position to be used in an anticompetitive manner.

Thus, courts in other parts of the world initiated cases concerning

Microsoft as a monopoly and some courts reached judgments affirming

that Microsoft was an illegal monopoly. In 2004, the European

Commission (EC) investigated Microsoft concerning its bundling of

the Windows operating system with the Windows Media Player

(WMP)as well as its practices around several server software products.[44]

Competitors to Windows Media Player asserted that this forced

bundling to the consumer was anticompetitive and was destroying the

market for their own products. The EC concluded in their

investigation "that the ubiquity which was immediately afforded to

WMP as a result of it being tied with the Windows PC OS artificially

reduces the incentives of music, film and other media companies, as

well software developers and content providers to develop their

---

[43] Eleanor M. Fox. Peterson Institute for International Economics, "US and EU
Competition Law: A Comparison" (Sept 27, 2011), p339.
[44] European Commission, "Cases>Microsoft",
http://ec.europa.eu/competition/sectors/ICT/microsoft/investigation.html
(December 15, 2015)

offerings to competing media players."[45] The EC found Microsoft in violation of EU laws and fined Microsoft €497 million ($666 million USD); a record fine at that time.[46] In 2007 the EC again found Microsoft in violation for their delay in implementing the 2004 order, and as a result ruled Microsoft to be a monopoly in two product categories and found Microsoft used that monopoly and abusive practices to stifle and/or eliminate competition. As a remedy, the EC imposed a new fine and additional remedies. While Microsoft accepted the initial decision and finding, the European antitrust regulators began investigating Microsoft again for failing to comply with the original 2004 order. In 2008, it fined Microsoft $1.3 billion and further reiterated that Microsoft continued to abuse its market dominance.[47]

In addition to the U.S. and the European Union, Microsoft was found to violate laws against illegal monopolies and/or anticompetitive practices in South Korea in 2005 and in Spain in 2011.

---

[45] European Commission, "Commission concludes on Microsoft investigation, imposes conduct remedies and a fine", http://europa.eu/rapid/press-release_IP-04-382_en.htm#file.tmp_Foot_2 (March 24, 2004).

[46] Free Software Foundation Europe, "European Commission vs Microsoft: chronology of the case", https://fsfe.org/activities/ms-vs-eu/timeline.en.html (December 15, 2015).

[47] Acohido, Byron, USA Today, "Microsoft apologizes for violating EU antitrust order", http://www.usatoday.com/story/tech/2013/03/06/microsoft-eu-antitrust-fine-731-million/1969007/ (March 6, 2013).

<u>Microsoft's operating system and Internet Explorer have exclusive</u>

<u>positioning in the marketplace creating an impossible barrier to entry</u>

Regardless of legal decisions or actions, advocates of the position that Microsoft was an illegal monopoly state that if Microsoft's operating systems and/or Internet Explorer had an exclusive position in the marketplace, then Microsoft was an illegal monopoly that was anticompetitive. Advocates believe this was validated with the findings of fact in *United States v. Microsoft.*

In *United States v. Microsoft,* the court issued findings of fact regarding the government's claim that Microsoft is an illegal monopoly. [48] The court concluded that:

1.) Microsoft's market share for personal computer operating systems is extremely large and stable,
2.) Microsoft's dominant market position is secured by a high barrier to entry, and
3.) The end result is that personal computer users lack a commercially viable alternative to its operating systems.

Bill Gates and Microsoft understood early that a computer was too complex of an object to be utilized by the vast number of personal and business users. It was their belief that standardizing the software

---

[48] United States Department of Justice, "U.S. V. Microsoft: Court's Findings Of Fact", http://www.justice.gov/atr/us-v-microsoft-courts-findings-fact (December 3, 2015).

that enabled the computers use was an absolute necessity to making personal computers mainstream.[49] To that end, their strategy was to produce an operating system that would become the standard of the industry and that instead of selling that operating system to end consumers, they would sell it to the computer manufacturer's to be included in all PC purchases. Microsoft began this strategy with MS-DOS. Microsoft purchased 86-DOS from Seattle Computer Products and its developer Tim Paterson in July 1981 and renamed the product MS-DOS.[50] By the end of the following year, Microsoft had licensed the product to more than 70 companies; including virtually all of the current personal computer manufacturers.[51] At the time, MS-DOS was not the only personal computer operating system. However, Gates clearly understood that placing MS-DOS on all personal computers through the OEM channel, he could standardize an entire industry.

Microsoft's objective of standardizing the industry on one operating system and a distribution strategy of selling product through

---

[49] Daniel Ichbiah. The Making of Microsoft: How Bill Gates and His Team Created the World. Danvers: Crown Publishing Group, 1991. P67-128.
[50] Antov, Leven, Digital Research, "History of MS-DOS", http://www.digitalresearch.biz/HISZMSD.HTM (May 6, 2015).
[51] Freiberger, Paul, InfoWorld, "Bill Gates, Microsoft and the IBM Personal Computer", (August 23, 1982), p.22.

the OEM channel was a success. From the time of the introduction of MS-DOS in the early 1980s and throughout the 1990s, Microsoft enjoyed a 90%+ market share in PC operating systems when measured by installed base.[52] With this large market share, companies competing in the PC operating system sector had little chance of selling directly to consumers since the Microsoft operating system was installed in all PC computers sent from the manufacturer.

Microsoft's belief from the start was that to make PCs mainstream, the operating system that enabled the computer had to be standardized. This strategy has been consistently cited by Bill Gates.[53] With a standardized operating system, independent software vendors (ISVs) could then write end-user applications that could run on any manufacturer's personal computer. Microsoft was correct. Since 90%+ of the PC market used Microsoft's operating system, ISVs would "write applications first and foremost to Windows, thereby ensuring a large body of applications from which consumers can choose."[54] According to Christopher Marsden author of *Regulating the*

[52]Moore, John Frederick, CNN Money, "MSFT ruled a monopoly", http://money.cnn.com/1999/11/05/technology/microsoft_finding/ (November 5, 1999).
[53] Ichbiah, p52-68.
[54] Marsden, Christopher, Regulating the Global Information Society (New York:

Global Information Society. Since other operating systems did not have this library of software produced by ISVs that was compatible with their operating system, this disadvantage to the consumer further consolidated Microsoft's market share dominance in operating systems.

The faction that believes Microsoft was an illegal monopoly concluded that due to this overwhelming dominance of the Microsoft operating system in the OEM channel, it was unrealistic to achieve and cost prohibitive to design, build, and market other operating systems for the Intel-based PC marketplace.

Microsoft uses its dominant market position to implement abusive practices to eliminate competition and stifle innovation

The advocates of this argument contend that Microsoft used its dominant market share to implement business practices that were specifically designed to stifle and/or eliminate competition in the operating system and web browser markets. Critics contend that "Microsoft was creating an unfair dominance in the PC software industry by bundling Microsoft's own web browser, Internet Explorer, within its Windows software package largely to undercut Netscape's browser".[55] As a direct result of Microsoft's dominant position in providing operating systems to the OEM channel, Microsoft was able to force personal computer makers to limit their ability to include Netscape Navigator, Opera or other web browsers as an option.

By the late 1990s to early 2000s, Microsoft had more than a 95% market share for web browsers based on web browser usage.[56] At issue was whether this success came from true consumer choice or through Microsoft's anticompetitive measures as a result of Microsoft's power distribution model. Critics of Microsoft contend that the consumer had no choice since Microsoft bundled the Internet Explorer with the Microsoft Windows operating system and used its monopoly position in the form of restrictive licensing agreements to force OEMs to support only its platform.[57] This rendered the consumer powerless to choose a product that might be better.

[55] American University, "Protecting Competition or Competitors? The Government's Double Edged Sword",
http://www1.american.edu/projects/mandala/TED/smith/Greenspoon.htm
(December 14, 2015).
[56] NetMarketShare, "Market Share Reports", http://marketshare.hitslink.com
(January 4, 2016).
[57] Hammond, R. Grant, Judicial Recusal: Principles, Process and Problems (New York: Hart Publishing, 2009), p43-55.

Critics point to Microsoft's dealing with Compaq as an example of where Microsoft abused its market dominance. This group contends that Microsoft abused its market dominance in operating systems in its dealings with Compaq computer over placement of the Internet Explorer and MSN icons on the desktop of computers shipped by Compaq. It was Compaq's intention to open its desktop to competing products and not to provide special treatment to Microsoft's Internet Explorer and MSN icons. Microsoft responded by sending Compaq a letter "stating its intention to terminate Compaq's license for Windows 95 if Compaq did not restore the MSN and Internet Explorer icons to their original positions."[58] As there was virtually no alternative market for operating systems, Compaq was forced to cede to Microsoft's demands rather than to risk losing the ability to license Windows 95. Critics contend that this was not an isolated event but rather an example of Microsoft's consistent behavior. During the trial of *U.S. v. Microsoft*, numerous witnesses including competitors and economists[59] gave examples of how

---

[58]Eisenach, Jeffrey A., Progress on Point, "The Microsoft Monopoly: The Facts, the Law and the Remedy", http://www.pff.org/issues-pubs/pops/pop7.4microsoftmonopolyfacts.html (April 2000) p1.

[59] John Wilke, Wall Street Journal, "Witness Cites Microsoft ` Monopoly Power", https://subscribe.wsj.com/microexamples/articlefiles/WitnessCitesMicrosoftMonopolyPower.doc (December 2, 1998)

Microsoft used its market dominance in operating systems to force OEMs to make decisions and policies that promoted Microsoft's products and stifled competition involving Apple, AOL, Real Networks and Sun Microsystems.[60]

Advocates believe the data clearly supports the position that Microsoft was an illegal monopoly that used its market dominance as a means to engage in anticompetitive behavior designed to stifle or eliminate competition. According to this view, Microsoft's success in these markets was not due to the company being more efficient or having a better product. Its success was instead tied to illegal monopolistic practices.

---

[60] Eisenach, p1.

View 2: Microsoft was not an illegal monopoly in the 1990s, merely an aggressive competitor with innovative products.

Advocates of this position believe that Microsoft critics have a fundamental lack of understanding of the marketplace where Microsoft was competing. They also contend that the judicial decisions often cited to support the view of Microsoft as an illegal monopoly were often overturned or their remedy eliminated due to market changes.

Judicial decisions and remedies changed over time indicating a lack of legal basis for determining that Microsoft was an illegal monopoly in the 1990s.

Advocates of the thesis that Microsoft was an illegal monopoly in the 1990s assert that one only has to look at the judicial record. Various judicial bodies determined that Microsoft was an illegal monopoly, therefore, Microsoft was an illegal monopoly. Critics of this argument contend that the issue is in fact much more complex. First, courts make mistakes and often correct themselves so they contend that historians must not look at the courts in a relatively small point of time as an absolute proof point. The U.S. judiciary has ruled on one side of a controversy at various times only to *correct* its position and take the other side of the controversy as time passed. In 1857 in the famous case *Dred Scott v. Sanford* the court ruled that slaves were property.[61] The 1896 case *Plessy v. Ferguson*, the U.S. Supreme Court ruled that requiring separate accommodations for blacks on train cars was not at odds with the equal protection under the laws clause of the Constitution.[62] The 1973 case of *Roe v. Wade* gave legal standing to the right of a female to choose to undergo an abortion procedure overturning many state laws and legal rulings. In all of these cases, the court made a decision that was later reversed or was reversing a previous flawed decision.

As with these famous judicial decisions that were later reversed, critics argue that many of the Microsoft rulings of illegal monopoly have already been overturned. In 2001, The U.S. Appeals Court overturned the 1999 previous antitrust ruling by Judge Penfield. This ruling went as far as ordering the judge removed from the case stating that he had "seriously tainted the proceedings."[63] The Microsoft

---

[61] Schultz, David, The Encyclopedia of the Supreme Court (New York: Infobase Publishing, 2005), p.132/

[62] Schultz, p148

[63] Brick, Michael, The New York Times, "U.S. Appeals Court Overturns Microsoft Antitrust Ruling", http://www.nytimes.com/2001/06/28/business/28WIRE-

breakup decree as a remedy for the court finding that Microsoft was an illegal monopoly never occurred. And, subsequent administrations believed that a breakup and a belief that Microsoft was an illegal monopoly was not accurate.[64]

Advocates for this side of the controversy conclude that merely looking at the legal decisions in a point of time does not either support or negate the underlying thesis of whether Microsoft was an illegal monopoly. Courts decisions change over time and both sides must look at the facts within an historical context.

Microsoft's market share in operating systems did not stifle nor prevent intense competition.

Microsoft and advocates for this side of the controversy contend that Microsoft had large market share in specific areas not because of anticompetitive practices but because its products were innovative and in high demand in a highly competitive marketplace. If it can be proved that consumers did have choice in a highly competitive and changing marketplace, the argument that Microsoft

---

SOFT.html (June 28, 2001).
[64] Keizer, Gregg, ComputerWorld, "The Microsoft breakup that never happened", http://www.computerworld.com/article/2497911/microsoft-windows/the-microsoft-breakup-that-never-happened.html (June 18, 2013).

was an illegal monopoly because the barrier to entry into the market was too great would fail.

The historical data indicates that Microsoft did in fact have a great deal of competition in many markets. During the late 1990s "Microsoft has only about 6% of the global software market and only 3% of the global computer market overall." [65] Existing at the time were many computer technology companies much larger than Microsoft including IBM, Sun Microsystems and Compaq.

In the operating system marketplace, there was an abundance of other operating systems, some of which were available at no charge to consumers. With this amount of consumer choice for feature and functionality as well as price point, critics of the position that Microsoft was an illegal monopoly find the proof point difficult to uphold. During the 1990s there was continued use of the UNIX operating system, growing popularity of the Linux operating system, and use of several proprietary operating systems from Apple and others.[66]

---

[65] "Microsoft And Windows Competitors",
http://www.123HelpMe.com/view.asp?id=77205 (January 18, 2016).
[66] Stephen White. "A Brief History of Computing
- Operating Systems",
http://trillian.randomstuff.org.uk/~stephen/history/timeline-OS.html (January 28, 2016).

The UNIX operating system started out as a file management system from Bell Labs in 1969.[67] Today it is still used due to its ability to operate a wide range of computers from personal computers to supercomputers. In fact, in some sectors of the server operating system market, UNIX had an impressive 40% market share in the late 1990s "Sun's high-end Unix server market share for systems costing more than $1 million grew to 40% in the third quarter of 1999 from 29% a year ago."[68]

LINUX is an open-source free operating system designed by Linus Torvalds and is based on the 1991 UNIX operating system. It has been developed and supported by hundreds of volunteers.[69] LINUX was the hot topic in the media in the late 1990s. A headline on CNET stated, "Linux closing in on Microsoft market share, study says".[70] That article further referenced a report from International

---

[67] Ceruzzi, Paul E., A History of Modern Computing (Boston: MIT Press, 2005) p.332.

[68] Vijayan, Jaikumar, Computerworld, "Sun Still Mines Gold from Unix Focus", http://www.computerworld.com/article/2593357/sun-still-mines-gold-from-unix-focus.html (January 31, 2000).

[69] Moody, Glyn, Rebel Code: The Inside Story of Linux and the Open Source Revolution (New York: Basic Books, 2002) p236.

[70] CNET, "Linux closing in on Microsoft market share, study says", http://www.cnet.com/news/linux-closing-in-on-microsoft-market-share-study-says/ (January 2, 2002).

Data Corp stating that the "free operating system will grab a bigger market share over the next few years".[71]

During the 1990s, the personal computer marketplace had fierce competition between PCs based on Microsoft Windows operating systems and Apple computers which used Apple's proprietary MacOS operating system. In the late 1990s, Apple had particular success in the laptop category. "The iBook and iMac dramatically helped Apple climb back to fame, doubling Apple's market share at the time to 11.2%."[72]

In addition to LINUX, UNIX, and MacOS, Microsoft had aggressive competition from a handful of others. Sun Microsystems had developed and was marketing the Solaris 8 operating system. Solaris 8, while not pre-installed on most PCs, was available on Sun's website. "Of the more than 1.2 million licenses for Solaris 8 that have been distributed through Sun's website, the vast majority have come from users putting Solaris on Intel systems, according to Sun."[73] End-

[71] CNET, "Linux closing in on Microsoft market share, study says", http://www.cnet.com/news/linux-closing-in-on-microsoft-market-share-study-says/ (January 2, 2002).
[72] LowEndMac, "Apple's Climb Back To Success, 1999-2001", http://lowendmac.com/2006/apples-climb-back-to-success-1999-to-2001/ (October 13, 2006).
[73] Vance, Ashlee, InfoWorld "Sun rethinks Solaris on Intel", (April 19, 2002), p1.

users with Intel based PCs were opting for Sun Solaris 8 instead of the pre-installed Microsoft operating system. IBM was offering its OS/2 Warp operating system. Even with the popularity of Microsoft Windows as the dominant pre-installed operating system on PCs, IBM's OS/2 still held as much as a 6% share of market in 1998.[74] Other operating systems marketed during this time included BeOS and AmigaOS.[75]

During this competitive time for operating systems, Bill Gates was convinced that standardizing the operating system was critical to bring personal computer technology to the masses. While critics contend he was anticompetitive, the evidence indicates that he encouraged other companies to utilize the same strategy; license their operating system to multiple hardware providers in a standardized fashion. This evidence was well documented by Eric Bruun in his book, *The Forbes Book of Great Business Letters:*

> In June of 1985, Bill Gates sent a remarkable memo to both the then-CEO of Apple, John Sculley, and then-head of Macintosh development, Jean Louis Gassée, and urged them to spread

---

[74] Green, Heather, BusinessWeek, "OS/2 vs. Windows, All Over Again", http://www.businessweek.com/microsoft/updates/up81117a.htm (November 17, 1998).
[75] White, p1

their wings by licensing their hardware and operating system to other companies.

Apple must make Macintosh a standard. But no personal computer company, not even IBM, can create a standard without independent support. Even though Apple realized this, they have not been able to gain the independent support required to be perceived as a standard.

Apple ignored his advice.

Five months after he sent the memo, Windows 1.0 was released. Microsoft's decision to do exactly as Gates had recommended to Apple resulted in market domination. Had Apple taken Gates' advice, things could have been so very different.

Steve Wozniak, Apple co-founder has since said: "The computer was never the problem. The company's strategy was. Apple saw itself as a hardware company; in order to protect our hardware profits, we didn't license our operating system. We had the most beautiful operating system, but to get it you had to buy our hardware at twice the price. That was a mistake. What we should have done was calculate an appropriate price to license the operating system. We were also naive to think that the best technology would prevail. It often doesn't."[76]

---

[76] "Letters of Note", http://www.lettersofnote.com/2012/02/apple-must-make-macintosh-standard.html (January 28, 2016).

During the 1990s, access of information through via the

Internet grew exponentially driven by the use of web browsers.[77] As

businesses and consumers realized the value of the worldwide web, the

browser marketplace became crucial as the entry point. In the web

browser marketplace, the 1990s saw what was coined the browser wars.[78]

Early in the 1990s, Netscape Navigator had a dominant market share.

Other browsers launched and used in the 1990s included IBM Web

Explorer, Navipress, SlipKnot, MacWeb, and Browse.[79] In 1995,

Microsoft introduced Internet Explorer. Those who argue that

Microsoft was an illegal monopoly have insisted that bundling Internet

Explorer with the various Microsoft Windows operating systems was

an illegal monopolistic practice that was anticompetitive in nature and

resulted in the inability for others to viably enter the marketplace. In

the legal proceedings by Netscape, the U.S. Dept. of Justice in the late

1990s, as well as the European Commission proceedings[80], these critics

---

[77] "Internet Growth Statistics",
http://www.internetworldstats.com/emarketing.htm (January 28, 2016).
[78] Levy, Robert, Cato Institute, "Microsoft and the Browser Wars: Fit to be Tied",
http://www.cato.org/publications/policy-analysis/microsoft-browser-wars-fit-be-tied (February 19, 1998)
[79] Quittner, Joshua, Speeding the Net: The Inside Story of Netscape and how it Challenged Microsoft (New York: Atlantic Monthly, 1998) p275-322.
[80] CNN Money, "Netscape sues Microsoft",
http://money.cnn.com/2002/01/22/technology/netscape/ (January 22, 2002).

point to the fact that Netscape was the dominant player with more than 90% market share prior to Microsoft entering the marketplace and that by 2002 Microsoft had replaced Netscape as the dominant leader with a 96% share of the marketplace.[81]

In the early 2000s, as Microsoft enjoyed market dominance in the browser marketplace, a second set of competitors emerged. AOL, which purchased Netscape in 1999, made available to open-source developers the code for Netscape Navigator.[82] The code was entrusted to a non-profit entity called the Mozilla Foundation. Mozilla Firefox 1.0 was released on November 9, 2004. It then continued to gain an increasing share of the browser market until it peaked in 2010.[83] Competition in the browser marketplace has continued with Google introducing Google Chrome in 2008.[84] According to Statcounter, as of December 2015 Google Chrome has a 53.6% market share, Internet Explorer 15.2%, Mozilla Firefox 14.3% and others 16.9%.[85]

---

[81] StatCounter, http://statcounter.com/
[82] Clark, Jim, Netscape Time: The Making of the Billion-Dollar Start-Up That Took on Microsoft (New York: St. Martin's Press, 2000) p52-68.
[83] StatCounter, http://statcounter.com/
[84] Wikipedia, "Google Chrome", https://en.wikipedia.org/wiki/Google_Chrome (January 4, 2016)
[85] StatCounter, http://statcounter.com/

In summary, the advocates that Microsoft was not an illegal monopoly believe that the evidence is compelling that most major legal rulings declaring Microsoft as an illegal monopoly have either been overturned or the remedy not implemented due to changing market conditions. They point to an analysis of the data showing compelling evidence that in fact the competition for operating systems and web browsers was intense and not stifled at all by Microsoft. In comparing the evidence and analysis of each position in the controversy a compelling conclusion is apparent.

Analysis and Conclusion

Upon review of both sides of the controversy, I conclude that Microsoft was not an illegal monopoly during the 1990s. Advocates that Microsoft was an illegal monopoly base their conclusions on the strongest two arguments: judicial bodies have concluded that Microsoft was an illegal monopoly, and Microsoft's dominant market share in operating systems made the barrier of entry for operating systems and web browsers impossible for viable competitors.

The judicial bodies have concluded argument fails as to logic and history. First, the argument commits argumentum ad verecundiam or fallacy of appeal to authority. Presuming that judicial bodies have the ultimate authority in reaching conclusion to a historical controversy eliminates the fact that the specific cases cited represent a small point of time in history. Judicial bodies routinely review and overturn decisions, as was the case of *United States v. Microsoft Corporation* 253 F.3d 34 (D.C. Cir. 2001). Sometimes history itself changes the foundation of arguments for a specific debate often resulting in judicial reconsideration over the longer term, many times decades, as is seen in many cases involving slavery and equal rights and the PC marketplace While historians should look at judicial actions for the proof points surfaced and discussed, historians should not automatically affirm one side of a controversy merely because a court has sided that way. Legal decisions change as history progresses and change. The judiciary is only one audience that supports one view of the controversy. They alone should not be the final arbiter of the controversy itself.

The next main argument in the controversy is that Microsoft was an illegal monopoly because Microsoft's dominant market share in operating systems created a barrier to entry that made it impossible for rival offerings to compete effectively in operating systems and web browsers. Microsoft's success recognizing trends in technology coupled with a core competency in technology distribution channels led to high market share and financial success. While Microsoft's success was the envy of its competitors, that success did not lock out new competitors who developed better technology or distribution channels and gave consumers a better choice.

District Judge Thomas Penfield Jackson wrote: "There are currently no products -- and there are not likely to be any in the near future -- that a significant percentage of computer users worldwide could substitute for Intel-compatible PC operating systems without incurring substantial costs."[86] However, an analysis of the data and subsequent history proves this assertion to be false. While Microsoft achieved enviable results in market share during the 1990s, they had significant competition from LINUX, UNIX, MacOS and others. In addition, their market share in operating systems did not provide them a dominant share of market in web browsers. Netscape Navigator had market share dominance during most of the 1990s. While Microsoft saw a brief market dominance in the early 2000s, it quickly eroded

---

[86] Jennings, Marianne, Business: Its Legal, Ethical, and Global Environment (Winfield: Southwestern College, 2010) p 534.

through the competitive efforts of Google Chrome and Mozilla Firefox.

Advocates of Microsoft was an illegal monopoly also assert that bundling the Internet Explorer with Microsoft's operating system created an illegal, anticompetitive environment. Robert Levy published this scenario in "Consumers Will Foot the Bill for Antitrust Remedies" *Legal Times*, April 5, 1999:

> "Consider the Washington Post as an analogy to Microsoft. The Post has a virtual monopoly in the Washington DC newspaper market. The Post "ties" its business section to the rest of the paper. When you buy the Post, one also gets the business section. Yet, the Post does not insist that its subscribers not buy competitive independent business publications like the Washington Business Journal. Imagine if the Post were forced by the government to untie its business section from the rest of the paper. (Levy, 1999: p22)."

The proposed remedy of breaking Microsoft apart was overturned by the court. And, history has shown that Microsoft's market share in both operating systems and web browsers has been substantially reduced not by government intervention. It has decreased through market competitiveness and consumer choice; often via technology paradigms and business models that did not even exist in the 1990s. As of 2015, Microsoft Windows' share of the market for operating systems on all computing devices -- PCs, smartphones, tablets, and all manner of hybrids -- stands at a modest 14%".[87]

In conclusion, the thesis that Microsoft was not an illegal monopoly in the 1990s but merely a successful innovator is affirmed. The fact that consumers chose to reward one company with high market share does not imply that other competitors do not exist and viable consumer choice does not exist. One company's success thereby creating a high barrier of entry does not imply an impossible barrier to entry. The data during the time period in question as well as the actual outcomes to Microsoft and the sector since the 1990s lead to a conclusion that supports the hypothesis.

---

[87] Preston, Rob, *InformationWeek*, "Microsoft Shows Tech 'Monopolies' Don't Last" http://www.informationweek.com/strategic-cio/digital-business/microsoft-shows-tech-monopolies-dont-last--/a/d-id/1297394 (July 18, 2014)

Bibliography

405 U.S. 596 (1972)",
https://supreme.justia.com/cases/federal/us/405/596/,
January 4, 2016.

Acohido, Byron. *USA Today*, "Microsoft apologizes for violating EU
antitrust order",
http://www.usatoday.com/story/tech/2013/03/06/microsoft-
eu-antitrust-fine-731-million/1969007/, March 6, 2013.

American University. "Protecting Competition or Competitors? The
Government's Double Edged Sword",
http://www1.american.edu/projects/mandala/TED/smith/G
reenspoon.htm, December 14, 2015.

Antov, Leven. *Digital Research*, "History of MS-DOS",
http://www.digitalresearch.biz/HISZMSD.HTM, May 6, 2015.

Bank, David. *Breaking Windows:* How Bill Gates Fumbled the Future of
Microsoft. New York: Free Press, 2007.

Berkun, Scott. *The Myths of Innovation.* Sebastopol: O'Reilly Media,
2007.

Brick, Michael. *The New York Times*, "U.S. Appeals Court Overturns
Microsoft Antitrust Ruling",
http://www.nytimes.com/2001/06/28/business/28WIRE-
SOFT.html, June 28, 2001.

Ceruzzi, Paul. *A History of Modern Computing.* Cambridge: MIT Press,
2003.

Clark, Jim. *Netscape Time:* The Making of the Billion-Dollar Start-Up
That Took on Microsoft. New York: St. Martin's Press, 2000.

Clay, Kelly. *Forbes*, "Why Microsoft's Layoff Is Much More Sweeping
Than The 18,000 Cuts"
http://www.forbes.com/sites/kellyclay/2014/07/20/microsof

t-layoffs-also-impact-thousands-of-contractors/#2715e4857a0be9941dc2c11a, July 20, 2014.

CNET. "IBM and Microsoft: Antitrust then and now", http://www.cnet.com/news/ibm-and-microsoft-antitrust-then-and-now/, January 2, 2002.

CNET. "Linux closing in on Microsoft market share, study says", http://www.cnet.com/news/linux-closing-in-on-microsoft-market-share-study-says/, January 2, 2002.

Collins Dictionary of Law. "monopoly", http://legal-dictionary.thefreedictionary.com/monopoly, December 3, 2015.

Eisenach, Jeffrey A. *Progress on Point*, "The Microsoft Monopoly: The Facts, the Law and the Remedy", http://www.pff.org/issues-pubs/pops/pop7.4microsoftmonopolyfacts.html, April 2000.

Encyclopaedia Britannica, "Clayton Antitrust Act", http://www.britannica.com/event/Clayton-Antitrust-Act, January 4, 2016.

European Commission, "Cases>Microsoft", http://ec.europa.eu/competition/sectors/ICT/microsoft/investigation.html, December 15, 2015.

Federal Trade Commission, "The Antitrust Laws", https://www.ftc.gov/tips-advice/competition-guidance/guide-antitrust-laws/antitrust-laws, December 4, 2015.

Financial Times, "Bill Gates on Microsoft", http://www.ft.com/cms/s/2/1674298c-fcbe-11da-9599-0000779e2340.html, June 15, 2006.

Free Software Foundation Europe, "European Commision vs Microsoft: chronology of the case", https://fsfe.org/activities/ms-vs-eu/timeline.en.html, December 15, 2015.

Freiberger, Paul. *InfoWorld*, "Bill Gates, Microsoft and the IBM Personal Computer", August 23, 1982.

Funk & Wagnalls Encyclopedia, "Monopoly", http://www.cosmeo.com, November 30, 2015.

Green, Heather. *BusinessWeek*, "OS/2 vs. Windows, All Over Again", http://www.businessweek.com/microsoft/updates/up81117a.htm, November 17, 1998.

Hammond, R. Grant. Judicial Recusal: *Principles, Process and Problems*, New York: Hart Publishing, 2009.

Ichbiah, Daniel et al. *The Making of Microsoft: How Bill Gates and His Team Created the World*. Danvers: Crown Publishing Group, 1991.

Jennings, Marianne. *Business: Its Legal, Ethical, and Global Environment*, Winfield: Southwestern College, 2010.

Jones, Capers. *The Technical and Social History of Software Engineering*. New York: Pearson Education, 2013.

Justia, U.S. Supreme Court, *"United States v. Topco Assocs., Inc"*, https://supreme.justia.com/cases/federal/us/405/596/case.html, December 4, 2015.

Kauffman, Kent. *Legal Ethics*, New York: Delmar Cengage Learning, 2008.

Keizer, Gregg. *ComputerWorld*, "The Microsoft breakup that never happened", http://www.computerworld.com/article/2497911/microsoft-windows/the-microsoft-breakup-that-never-happened.html, June 18, 2013.

Kempf Jr., Donald G. *The Seattle Times*, "Antitrust Upside Down: The Microsoft Case.", October 11 1999.

Law Library - *American Law and Legal Information*. "Monopoly – Government Regulation", http://law.jrank.org/pages/8632/Monopoly-Government-Regulation.html, December 15, 2015.

Legal Information Institute. "*15 U.S. Code § 1 - Trusts, etc., in restraint of trade illegal; penalty*", https://www.law.cornell.edu/uscode/text/15/1, January 4, 2016.

Legal Information Institute. "*15 U.S. Code § 13 - Discrimination in price, services, or facilities*", https://www.law.cornell.edu/uscode/text/15/13, January 4, 2016.

Legal Information Institute. "*U.S. Code: Title 49 - TRANSPORTATION* ", https://www.law.cornell.edu/uscode/text/49/, January 4, 2016.

Legal Information Institute. "*15 U.S. Code Subchapter I - FEDERAL TRADE COMMISSION*", https://www.law.cornell.edu/uscode/text/15/chapter-2/subchapter-I, January 4, 2016.

Legal Information Institute. "*15 U.S. Code § 12 - Definitions; short title*", https://www.law.cornell.edu/uscode/text/15/12, January 4, 2016.

Levy, Robert. Cato Institute. "*Microsoft and the Browser Wars: Fit to be Tied*", http://www.cato.org/publications/policy-analysis/microsoft-browser-wars-fit-be-tied, February 19, 1998.

Lohr, Steve. *The New York Times*. "Judge Clears Antitrust Pact For Microsoft", http://www.nytimes.com/1995/08/22/business/judge-clears-antitrust-pact-for-microsoft.html, August 22, 1995.

Lowe, Janet. *Bill Gates Speaks: Insight from the World's Greatest Entrepreneur.* Hoboken: Wiley, 1998.

LowEndMac, "Apple's Climb Back To Success, 1999-2001", http://lowendmac.com/2006/apples-climb-back-to-success-1999-to-2001/, October 13, 2006.

Manes, Stephen et al. *Gates: How Microsoft's Mogul Reinvented an Industry--and Made Himself.* New York City: Touchstone, 1992.

Marsden, Christopher. *Regulating the Global Information Society*, New York: Routledge, 2005.

"*Microsoft And Windows Competitors*", http://www.123HelpMe.com/view.asp?id=77205, January 18, 2016.

Moody, Glyn. *Rebel Code: The Inside Story of Linux and the Open Source Revolution*, New York: Basic Books, 2002.

Moore, John Frederick. *CNN Money*, "MSFT ruled a monopoly", http://money.cnn.com/1999/11/05/technology/microsoft_finding/, November 5, 1999.

Musolf, Nell. *The Story of Microsoft.* Mankato: Creative Company, 2008.

NetMarketShare. "*Market Share Reports*", http://marketshare.hitslink.com, January 4, 2016.

New World Encyclopedia contributors. *New World Encyclopedia*, "Microsoft", http://www.newworldencyclopedia.org/p/index.php?title=Microsoft&oldid=980539, January 22, 2016.

Preston, Rob. *InformationWeek*, "Microsoft Shows Tech 'Monopolies' Don't Last" http://www.informationweek.com/strategic-cio/digital-business/microsoft-shows-tech-monopolies-dont-last--/a/d-id/1297394, July 18, 2014.

Quittner, Joshua. *Speeding the Net: The Inside Story of Netscape and how it Challenged Microsoft*, New York: Atlantic Monthly, 1998.

Schultz, David. The Encyclopedia of the Supreme Court, New York: Infobase Publishing, 2005.

StatCounter, http://statcounter.com/

United States Department of Justice, *"U.S. v. Microsoft: Court's Findings Of Fact"*, http://www.justice.gov/atr/us-v_microsoft-courts-findings-fact, December 3, 2015.

United States Department of Justice, *"Antitrust Laws and You"*, http://www.justice.gov/atr/antitrust-laws-and-you, December 3, 2015.

United States of America, *Appellee v. Microsoft Corporation*, Appellant, 253 F.3d 34 (D.C. Cir. 2001), Justia U.S. Law, http://law.justia.com/cases/federal/appellate-courts/F3/253/34/576095/, December 30, 2015.

Vance, Ashlee. *InfoWorld* "Sun rethinks Solaris on Intel", April 19, 2002.

Vijayan, Jaikumar. *Computerworld*, "Sun Still Mines Gold from Unix Focus", http://www.computerworld.com/article/2593357/sun-still-mines-gold-from-unix-focus.html, January 31, 2000.

Wallace, James. *Hard Drive: Bill Gates and the Making of the Microsoft Empire.* New York: HarperCollins, 1992.

Wikipedia, "Google Chrome", https://en.wikipedia.org/wiki/Google_Chrome, January 4, 2016.

Wikipedia, "Microsoft litigation", https://en.wikipedia.org/wiki/Microsoft_litigation#Anti-trust, December 2, 2015.

Wired Magazine, "U.S. v. Microsoft: Timeline", http://www.wired.com/2002/11/u-s-v-microsoft-timeline/, November 4, 2002.

World Heritage Encyclopedia, "Microsoft litigation", http://www.worldheritage.org/articles/Microsoft_litigation, December 15, 2015.

Yahoo Finance, "MSFT",
http://finance.yahoo.com/q/ks?s=MSFT+Key+Statistics,
November 2, 2015.

Yin, Robert. *Case Study Research: Design and Methods (Applied Social Research Methods)* Paperback. Thousand Oaks: Sage Publications, 2013.

www.ingramcontent.com/pod-product-compliance
Lightning Source LLC
Chambersburg PA
CBHW061038050326
40689CB00012B/2881